Prepare Him Room

Robert Martin Walker

Prepare
Him Room

An Advent Study for Adults

Abingdon Press / Nashville

PREPARE HIM ROOM:
AN ADVENT STUDY FOR ADULTS

Copyright © 2000 by Robert Martin Walker

This book is printed on acid-free paper.

Library of Congress Cataloging-in-Publication Data

Walker, Robert Martin.
    Prepare Him room: an Advent study for adults / Robert Martin Walker.
        p. cm.
    ISBN 0-687-09026-1 (alk. paper)
    1. Advent--Prayer-books and devotions--English. I. Title.

BV40 .W26 2000
242'.332--dc21

00-058266

Scripture quotations, unless otherwise noted, are from the *Holy Bible: New Revised Standard
Version*, copyright © 1989, by the Division of Christian Education of the National Council of
the Churches of Christ in the United States of America. Used by permission. All rights
reserved.

That noted RSV is from the *Holy Bible: Revised Standard Version*, copyright © 1946, 1952, 1959,
1973 by the Division of Christian Education of the National Council of the Churches of
Christ in the U.S.A. Used by permission. All rights reserved.

00 01 02 03 04 05 06 07 08 09 — 10 9 8 7 6 5 4 3 2 1

MANUFACTURED IN THE UNITED STATES OF AMERICA

*For Aunt Sis and Uncle Charlie,
with deepest love and admiration*

Contents

Introduction

Advent is a time to prepare our hearts and minds to meet Jesus Christ. A phrase from the familiar hymn *Joy to the World* underlines this truth: "Let every heart prepare him room...."

We can meet Christ in a multitude of ways and in a variety of places. Christ is present in the ecstasy of victory and in the agony of disappointment. We can encounter Christ in the mundane routines of daily life as well as the high moments of worship. Christ meets us in noisy times of celebration and in quiet moments of prayer and meditation.

Where and when we meet Christ—or where and when *we are met by* Christ—is not the most important issue. The significant issue is *that* we encounter Christ in some time and some place.

While we can discover Christ in the mundane, everyday routines of living, we also encounter Christ in the extremes of life—birth and death, agony and ecstasy, tragedy and triumph. These extremes can be thought of as a "boundary" or an "edge" at the outer limits of life. Meeting Christ at these edges can be a powerful, transforming experience.

Many of life's edges can be expressed as polar opposites: joy / sorrow; pain / relief; despair / hope; life / death. Christ is surely present at all times, but we become more keenly aware of this presence when we are up against one of life's edges.

Here is one example that can illustrate this point. When my grandmother died several years ago, I officiated at her funeral. This was a time of loss and sadness for our family. I wasn't sure if I could get through the sermon without breaking down. However, when I began to speak the words of resurrection and new life, I felt a sense of peace and reassurance that bordered on joy. I realize now that Christ was present at the edges of sorrow and joy.

I believe that all of us, if we search our memories, will discover similar experiences. The late theologian Paul Tillich contended that God's grace "strikes" us when we're in great pain and restlessness. Tillich's observation highlights yet two more of life's edges: grace / restlessness.

One important characteristic of edges is that they are points of decision. At an edge, we must decide which way to turn or whether to proceed straight ahead. At these edges, we can turn toward Christ or we can turn away; we can choose to recognize Christ's presence or we can decide to ignore him.

This Advent study will explore four sets of edges: promise / fulfillment; despair / hope; sadness / joy; death / birth. I have picked these in large part because they are themes of the Advent season. However, these particular edges are common to all of our lives at one time or another.

My great hope is that over these four weeks, you will learn to recognize the edges in your own life as well as where Christ is present in them. May Advent be a time for you to prepare your heart to meet Jesus Christ.

Robert Martin Walker

Promise / Fulfillment

Scripture: Read Isaiah 9:2-7.

I Have Promises to Keep...

When one of my sons was five years old, I promised him that I would take him to the American Museum of Natural History in New York City the next Saturday. He and his brother loved this museum, which they called "the Whale-on-the-Ceiling Museum," referring to a life-size replica of a giant blue whale that hung from the ceiling of one of the museum's cavernous rooms. All during the week, my son eagerly anticipated going to the museum, asking me every day, "Is this the day?"

When Saturday came, I received a morning phone call from the local hospital telling me that one of the members of my church was having emergency heart surgery. After making a quick apology to my disappointed son, I rushed to the hospital. Because of the length of the surgery (four hours), by the time I got home it was too late to go to the museum.

My son was crushed. He kept crying, "But you promised, Dad!" He was too young to understand the concept of priorities and that some promises are superseded by emergencies. All he knew was his disappointment at not being able to go where I had promised to take him.

Most of us don't take promises lightly. Neither should we

make promises casually. To give a promise is to give someone your word. To break a promise is to risk losing credibility. When someone repeatedly doesn't fulfill their promises, then we no longer trust them.

Advent: Promises, Promises

Advent is a many-faceted season. Culturally, it's a time of preparing for Christmas by shopping for presents, going to holiday parties, getting ready for family to visit, or making preparations for travel.

Advent also ushers in the end of the year. For businesses, this can mean extra hours of work. For many students, semester final exams come during Advent. The four weeks before Christmas can be the busiest time of the year.

As a religious season, Advent is a time of preparing ourselves for the coming of Christ. As the Scriptures make clear, we live between the first coming of Christ and the final coming of Christ. Yet as the Scriptures also make clear, Christ doesn't come only twice; Christ comes again and again into our lives and into the world. In the words of John in exile in Patmos, Christ is the one "who is and who was and who is to come" (Revelation 1:8).

The promise of Advent is threefold: Christ has come! Christ is coming! Christ will come again! The issue for us is whether we will believe these promises and live in light of them.

Living Between the "Already" and the "Not Yet"

The late theologian Karl Barth spoke of Christian existence as living between the "already" and the "not yet." That is, Christ has already come in Jesus of Nazareth. This "first" coming was the fulfillment of Old Testament promises that God would send a Messiah to redeem the world. However, the reign of God that

Jesus ushered in is not yet fully established. This kingdom of love, justice, and peace foretold by the prophets, especially Isaiah, has been inaugurated but not fulfilled.

When you think about it, our daily lives are lived between the already and the not yet. For instance, we give and receive love with members of our families and our friends. Such love is "already" present. However, this love is dynamic—it changes and grows over time. The love we share with those closest to us is always moving toward fulfillment. This love is "not yet" fulfilled.

John Wesley's concept of "Christian perfection" is instructive here. Wesley believed that it was possible for a person to become "perfect" in love. He understood that the goal of sanctification (growth in holiness) was perfection. However, Wesley believed that perfection was a moving target. We can never say, "I've achieved perfection, and I can't grow any more." Rather, we say, "I'm moving toward perfection."

One of the questions asked of those ordained as United Methodist ministers is, "Are you going on to perfection?" This question comes directly from Wesley's writings. During my ordination service, Bishop W. McFerrin Stowe paused after asking this question because there was some nervous laughter among the ordinands. He asked, "If you're not going on to perfection, then where are you going?" Perfection in love is a direction rather than a destination.

A Special Type of Promise: Covenant

Making promises is a regular feature of our lives. Some of these promises are, in their own way, small: "I'll mow the lawn right after the football game"; "I'll pick up a gallon of milk on my way home." We make many of these minor promises each day.

But we also make big promises such as taking on a mortgage (a promise to pay back a typically large amount of borrowed money), getting married, or signing employment contracts. The bigger the promise, the greater the consequences for breaking it.

Religiously speaking, a big promise is called a covenant. A covenant is an agreement between two parties. There are several well-known covenants in the Bible. There is the Abrahamic covenant between God and the people of Israel. There is the Noahic covenant, in which God promised never again to destroy the earth with a flood. There is the Davidic covenant, in which was promised a Messiah / King from David's lineage. There is also the "new covenant" outlined by Jeremiah (31:31), in which God promised to write the law of God on our hearts.

These covenants involved promises made by one party to the other or by both parties to each other. For instance, in the Abrahamic covenant, God promised to be Israel's God and Israel promised to live and act as God's people.

One description of Christians is that we are "a covenant people." Not only are we a part of God's covenants with people throughout the Scriptures, we are part of a "baptismal covenant." When we are baptized, we take vows to oppose evil and be faithful to God through Jesus Christ. In baptism, we also promise to be faithful supporters of the church in its mission. The vows we take at baptism are among the largest promises we make.

A Messiah Is Promised

During Advent, we hear Scriptures that tell of God's promise to send a Messiah to redeem the world. Isaiah 9:2-7, cited at the beginning of this chapter, contains such a promise. Isaiah prophesies a new age in which the world moves from darkness to light, from oppression to freedom, and from war to peace. A "child" endowed with God's authority will rule in this new age of peace and justice. This ruler will be the promised Messiah who will sit on David's throne (Isaiah 9:7).

Isaiah 9:2-7 echoes the Davidic covenant, as does Isaiah 11:1-9. These passages are traditionally read during Advent to remind Christians of how Old Testament prophecies point to Jesus Christ. We believe that these promises of God are fulfilled in Jesus.

The stories of Jesus' birth in Matthew and Luke show how the events surrounding Jesus' birth and the birth itself fulfill Old Testament prophecies. Matthew's Gospel does this explicitly, citing Old Testament passages several times, using some variation of the words "this took place in order to fulfill what had been spoken through the prophet...." In each step of Jesus' birth, Matthew sees the fulfillment of messianic prophecies.

Whether or not we see Jesus as the promised Messiah comes down to one decision: faith. Will we believe that God's promises of a Savior were fulfilled in Jesus? This crucial question is put to us during Advent with great urgency.

The Promise of Abundant Life

Christ promises us the rich, full, and abundant life of faith. "I came that they might have life and have it abundantly" is one well-known form of Christ's promise. (See John 10:10.) Often, the fulfillment of this promise seems elusive. A devastating illness or the tragic death of someone we love can lead us to question this promise. Suffering an injustice can cause us to doubt the promise of abundant life.

During difficult and challenging times in our lives, we can easily wonder, "What happened to the promise of abundant life?" The gospel reassures us that the promise of abundant life stands firm no matter what our personal difficulties. Christ's presence can strengthen our resolve and determination in the midst of tough times.

In many respects, the world of the first century was similar to our world. Jesus was born into a world raging with violence, discord, poverty, and oppression. The destructive forces of evil were present in Jesus' society. Into this world came the promise of salvation and abundant life. It is by faith that we today claim this promise and cling to it tightly in life's challenging moments.

Living on the Edge of Fulfillment

In personal terms, fulfillment can seem elusive. Like Wesley's concept of "perfection," fulfillment is a moving target. A pastor friend of mine would say at the beginning of each year, "I believe that this is the year we're going to get it together in the church." This hope expressed both his optimism about the church's future and the reality that "getting it together" is always beyond our reach.

Perhaps we need to understand that "fulfillment" is part of the journey rather than a destination. We can never say, "We've arrived," in the sense that fulfillment is fully here. However, we can learn to be content in a variety of circumstances.

Paul wrote in Philippians 4:11-13:

I have learned to be content with whatever I have. I know what it is to have little, and I know what it is to have plenty. In any and all circumstances I have learned the secret of being well-fed and of going hungry, of having plenty and of being in need. I can do all things through Christ who strengthens me.

Contentment is a state of the mind and spirit more than it is a condition of fulfillment of bodily needs. This is why we can be well fed and prosperous but also miserable. Fulfillment is based on what is going on inside of us rather than the circumstances of life. Granted, difficult circumstances test our inner peace and joy. However, Paul reminds us of Christ's strengthening presence.

Waiting For Fulfillment

Samuel Beckett's play "Waiting for Godot" centers on a conversation between friends waiting for another friend. Their conversation pertains to the arriving friend, Godot, and what will happen when he comes. However, Godot never arrives, making the friends' talk meaningless.

When you think about it, much of life is spent waiting. We wait in lines to see movies, to buy clothes and groceries, and to purchase "fast food." We wait for friends to return our calls or e-mails and for family members to arrive for holidays. In a deeper sense, life is waiting.

Some of our waiting is anxious and restless, as when we are waiting to hear the results of a biopsy. At other times, waiting is boring, as when we're "killing time." Waiting can be a difficult experience, especially if we become impatient.

We also wait for the fulfillment of promises. If someone vows to meet us at a certain time and place and doesn't show up, we are understandably irritated. During Advent, we engage in a special kind of waiting—waiting for Christ to come. The word *Advent* means "to come." Christ's first coming at Bethlehem was the fulfillment of messianic prophecies in the Old Testament. Christ's final coming is a future hope. However, Christ doesn't come to us only twice; Christ comes again and again.

When we look at life with the eyes of faith, we can see that Christ is always coming into our lives and our world. Our task is to be open and receptive to these "comings."

Study and Discussion Questions

1. When have you been on the receiving end of a broken promise? How did you feel? When have you had to break a promise you made? How did the person to whom you made the promise react?
2. In what ways has Christ come into your life? How do these "comings" fulfill the promise that Christ is the one "who is coming, who has come, and who will come"?
3. Visualize the first time you realized you loved someone. Then reflect on how your love for that person has changed over the years. Can love grow over a lifetime? Explain your answer.
4. What "everyday" covenants do you make? What are the "big" covenants in your life? What covenants are implied in these relationships: marriage, parenting, employment, church membership?
5. In what ways does Jesus' birth fulfill the promises contained in Isaiah 9:2-7? How did Jesus' words and actions fulfill the roles of "Wonderful Counselor" and "Prince of Peace" (Isaiah 9:6)? In what ways did Jesus' life establish justice and righteousness (9:7)?
6. When do you most need to be reassured of the promise of abundant life? How has Christ been present with you in times when the promise of abundant life has seemed distant?

7. What is your reaction to Paul's statement in Philippians 4:11-13? Do you believe that it is possible to be content in "any and all circumstances"? Why or why not?

8. For what do you have difficulty waiting? What makes waiting a restless and anxious time? When have you waited patiently? What does it mean to wait for Christ's coming?

Deepening Your Advent Journey

- Make a list of promises that you have received. Put these promises into three categories: "Promises Made to Me by Others," "Promises I've Made to Myself," and "Promises Made to Me by God." After making this list, reflect on it using these questions: Which promises are most important? Which promises have been kept? Which promises have been broken? Which promises are yet to be fulfilled?

- Think about a promise you made to another person, a promise that you haven't yet fulfilled. If possible, follow through and fulfill that promise this week.

- One of the ways we prepare for Christmas is by buying gifts. Because so many other people are doing the same thing, we spend more time waiting in lines and in traffic during December. Practice waiting patiently by creatively using your waiting time. While you are waiting, you might reflect on the presence of Christ in your life or pray for those who are waiting with you.

Second Week of Advent

Despair / Hope

Scripture: Read Isaiah 40:1-5.

The Despair Called Exile

In 587 B.C., the Babylonian King Nebuchadnezzar ordered the deportation of many young, strong, rebellious Israelites to Babylon. A fifty-year period of exile in Babylon followed. Nebuchadnezzar's cruel strategy for subduing the Israelites worked; there were no more rebellions.

While the Exile resulted in some benefits to God's people (most notably, many parts of the Old Testament were put in written form to preserve them for future generations and the synagogue came into being), it was also a time of despair. The Hebrews were a people of the land. The Promised Land had been given to them by God as part of the covenant with Abraham to make of them a great nation.

Psalm 137 captures the misery of the exiled Hebrews:

> By the rivers of Babylon—
> > there we sat down and there we wept
> > when we remembered Zion.
> ....
> For there our captors
> > asked us for songs.
> ....
> How could we sing the LORD's song
> > in a foreign land? (Psalm 137:1, 3-4)

In this hymn, you can hear the Hebrews' anguish over being separated from their beloved homeland. God's people had been wrenched from their homeland and now had to exist in a foreign place with a different language, customs, and religion. The exiles were living on the edge of despair.

Advent Can Be a SAD Time

The cultural myth about the weeks before and including Christmas is that this is "the most wonderful time of the year," as the popular song goes. Feel-good movies like *It's a Wonderful Life* and *Miracle on 34th Street* appear relentlessly on TV schedules during December. Shopping malls and grocery stores are filled with the music of holiday carols and decorations.

To buy into the cultural myth about Christmastime is to believe that we should be constantly giddy with the joy of the holiday season. Yet, the reality is far darker than the myth. Christmas can be a difficult and depressing time, especially for persons who have lost a loved one to death. Sharing a holiday alone can be lonely and sad. And believing that everyone else is having a great time only adds to the unhappiness we might be feeling.

Depression actually increases during Christmastime. Sadness during December is so pervasive that psychologists have invented a name for it: Seasonal Affective Disorder (SAD). While there are several theories for why depression is higher in the winter (it may have to do with our generally receiving less sunlight during this season), it's difficult to deny the reality of Christmas being a time of sadness, even despair, for some people.

The Lament: Poetry of Despair

It may surprise you to learn that the most common type of psalm is the lament. Individual and community laments account for more than one third of the 150 psalms. Most laments are in the form of a plea or petition for God's help. When we're in despair over our situation, our prayer to God is a desperate lament.

Psalm 13 is a prime example of a lament.

How long, O LORD? Will you forget me forever?
  How long will you hide your face from me?
How long must I bear pain in my soul,
  and have sorrow in my heart all day long? (verses 1-2)

Like the other psalms of lamentation, Psalm 13 ends with a note of hope:

I will sing to the LORD,
  because he has dealt bountifully with me. (verse 6)

This psalm of lament, filled with the poetry of despair, makes the movement from despair to hope and affirmation. While the psalmist begins with despair and a plea for help, there is an acknowledgment of God's goodness, love, and power. This movement from despair to hope is one of the movements of a life of faith in God.

Hope for the Exiles

The Book of Isaiah contains the writings of at least two authors. The first, Isaiah of Jerusalem, prophesied more than a century before the Exile. The second author, sometimes called "Deutero-Isaiah" or "Second Isaiah," prophesied many years later, toward the end of the Exile. Second Isaiah's writings begin in chapter 40 and continue at least through chapter 55. These chapters also contain four "suffering servant" songs, in which the writers of the New Testament found prophecies pointing to Jesus.

Second Isaiah beings with a word of comfort and hope:

Comfort, O comfort my people,
   says your God.
Speak tenderly to Jerusalem,
   and cry to her
that she has served her term. (Isaiah 40:1-2)

The "term" in the above verse refers to the Exile. Chapter 40 of Isaiah goes on to describe a glorious return from the Babylonian exile on a "desert highway," paved by leveling mountains and lifting up valleys. The entire chapter is a joyful celebration of exiles returning to the Holy Land God had given to them. Second Isaiah describes this "new thing"— God's redeeming the exiles—as a glorious time of hope and fulfillment (see 43:19).

Grace "Strikes" Us in Our Despair

Reflecting on my life, I have come to realize that genuine hope comes when I am mired in the darkness of despair. Hope is a light in the darkness that shows us the way out of depression, disappointment, and despair. Alcoholics Anonymous teaches that persons often have to "hit bottom" before they will accept the fact that they are powerless to overcome their alcoholism by sheer individual effort. When it comes to faith in Christ, a similar principle applies: When we give up trying to save ourselves, then we are open to the saving power of Jesus Christ.

In a sermon titled "You Are Accepted," the theologian Paul Tillich preached the following words.

Grace strikes us when we are in great pain and restlessness. It strikes us when we walk through the dark valley of a meaningless and empty life. It strikes us when we feel that our separation is deeper than usual...when our indifference, our weakness, our hostility, and our lack of direction and composure have become intolerable to us....Sometimes at that moment a wave of light breaks into our darkness, and it is as though a voice were saying, "You are accepted."

(The Shaking of the Foundations.
Charles Scribner's Sons, 1948, pages 161–62)

When we are on the edge of despair, God's grace can "strike" us as a light in the darkness. This "light" can lead us from despair to hope.

Jesus and the Man Who Was Paralyzed

The story of Jesus healing a man who was paralyzed (Matthew 9:2-8) is an excellent example of the movement from despair to hope. In Jesus' time, being paralyzed meant being completely dependent on others for food, shelter, and care. There were no wheelchairs or other devices to help provide persons who were physically disabled with independence of movement. This man's friends, because of their concerns for and loyalty to him, decide to carry him to Jesus for healing.

We can identify with this man in Matthew 9 not only in terms of his physical disability. There are other ways to be paralyzed. Most often, what paralyzes us in nonphysical ways is fear. When we are afraid, we would rather not make decisions or take actions. One classic metaphor for this kind of paralysis is the story of Lot's wife (Genesis 19), who was torn between fleeing the destruction of Sodom and longing for her life there. She was "paralyzed"—turned into a pillar of salt as a symbol of her inability to go forward or turn back.

To be paralyzed emotionally or spiritually can be a cause of hopelessness. When you don't have the will and energy to move forward in any area of life, paralysis can be a source of despair.

Healing and Hope

Returning to the story of Jesus and the man who was paralyzed, when the man was brought to Jesus, Jesus' first words to him were, "Take heart, son; your sins are forgiven" (Matthew 9:2). These words are surprising. We would expect Jesus to say something like, "Stand up, take your bed and go to your home" (see 9:6). Instead, Jesus first offers the man forgiveness.

What Jesus offered to this man in Matthew 9 is nothing less than full healing. Jesus offered the man wholeness through a new relationship of love and forgiveness with God. This "inner" healing of forgiveness is also what Jesus offers us in our emotional and spiritual paralyses.

The words "you are forgiven" are the most hopeful words we can hear. When we are laboring under a burden of guilt over things we have done and things we should have done but didn't, we can despair of ever being whole and free. Someone has said of guilt, "It's a gift that keeps on giving." Guilt has a way of gnawing away at our spirits until all that remains is discontentment, unhappiness, and fear of facing our sins. As the psalmist wrote, "When I kept silence, my body wasted away / through my groaning all the day long" (Psalm 32:3). Forgiveness heals us by making whole a life torn apart by guilt.

With forgiveness comes hope for a new and restored relationship with God, others, and self. Once the crushing burden of guilt is lifted, we need not be "paralyzed"; we are free to live the full and abundant life God wants for us.

Horizons of Hope

Advent is a prime time for looking toward horizons. During these weeks before Christmas, we look back to the distant horizon of Jesus' birth. We also look forward to the far horizon of Christ's final coming and the fulfillment of time. And we look to the nearer horizon of upcoming Christmas celebrations. Looking toward any of these horizons can be a source of hope.

The horizon behind us—Jesus' birth—brings hope to us through the Savior who came to redeem us. Jesus' birth, death, and resurrection bring hope to a world longing for forgiveness and redemption. The thought that God loved us enough to become incarnate is uplifting. To know that we are loved so much brings light into the darkness of our lives.

The horizon far ahead—Jesus' final coming—is also a source of hope. When we know that the future is in God's hands, we can live more confidently in the present. The belief that God will bring our world and history to some kind of fulfillment offers us reassurance about the future.

The horizon immediately ahead—Christmas—can fill us with anticipation and even excitement. The traditions of celebrating the birth of a Savior are both familiar and comforting. The carols we sing lift our spirits, and the Christmas story has the power to inspire hope in us.

By looking toward these three horizons, Advent helps us encounter Christ as past event, future hope, and present reality. Anytime we encounter Christ, hope is born in us.

Study and Discussion Questions

1. When have you felt exiled from your true home? What emotions did you experience during this "exile"?
2. What examples of the "cultural myth of Christmas" do

you see around you? When have you been unhappy during the Christmas season? What led to your unhappiness?

3. Why do you think that the lament is the most common type of psalm? In what ways do you identify with Psalm 13?

4. If you had been a Hebrew in Babylonian exile, how do you think you might have reacted to hearing the words in Isaiah 40? Would Isaiah's prophecy be enough to lift you from the despair of being separated from your homeland? In what way does Isaiah 40 speak to you today?

5. When have you been "struck" by God's grace? How did grace bring hope and light into a situation of despair and darkness?

6. When have you felt "paralyzed" by circumstances in your life? What happened to you emotionally and spiritually during this time?

7. When have you been on the receiving end of forgiveness? When have you been on the giving end of forgiveness? How did forgiveness change your relationship with the other person?

8. Of the three horizons mentioned earlier, which one is most important to you during Advent? How does looking toward these horizons inspire hope in you?

Deepening Your Advent Journey

• Read Psalm 137, a lament of the Israelites exiled in Babylon. Imagine yourself in the place of one of these exiles. You have been taken from your home, your land, and your family. It is unlikely that you'll ever return. Get in touch with the feelings of loss and sadness that would accompany such an exile. Then explore the question, "Where is God in this experience?"

- Reread Isaiah 40:1-5, looking for the hopeful images contained in this passage. On a sheet of paper, make a list of these images of hope, and take a few minutes to reflect on them and what they say to you in your own circumstances.
- Think back over your life and remember a time of despair. What was the source of that despair? What circumstances, internal and external, led to feelings of despair, disappointment, and loss? What were your spiritual issues in this time of despair? Then, remember what brought hope to you during this time. How did your faith in God strengthen you? What led to the healing of your despair?
- In the next week, reach out to a person who seems to be having a difficult time coping with the holiday season. Some people experience Christmas as an unhappy time for a variety of reasons: memories of loved ones lost through death, a feeling of being left out of the joy of Christmas, or guilt over not being happier about Christmastime. Visit this person and take along a small gift, like cookies or an ornament, to brighten the darkness of the holidays. Of course, the most important gift you can give is that of your time and care.

Sadness / Joy

Scripture: Read Psalm 126.

A Time to Weep, a Time to Laugh

The author of the Book of Ecclesiastes was a teacher / scholar who was also a keen observer of life. In his lifetime, he was on a quest for wisdom, seeking it through wealth, pleasure, and friendships. Each of these avenues proved to be a dead end, and the author pronounces as "vanity" anyone's seeking genuine fulfillment through them.

In his quest for wisdom, the "Teacher" (a translation of the Hebrew word *Koheleth*) reaches some conclusions about life, truth, and happiness. One of those conclusions is expressed in chapter 3 of the Book of Ecclesiastes: "For everything there is a season, and a time for every matter under heaven" (3:1). The Teacher goes on to write that there is

> a time to weep, and a time to laugh;
> a time to mourn, and a time to dance. (3:4)

Weeping and laughing are two edges of life that we all experience. Who hasn't tasted the salt of tears running down cheeks in a time of sadness? And who hasn't known laughter during times of joy?

The Teacher, however, is making a crucial point: Both

weeping and laughing are in the realm of God's care. There is a time and a purpose for both in the kingdom of God.

Jesus Enters Into Our Pain

In the Letter to the Hebrews, Jesus is portrayed as a high priest who intercedes with God on our behalf. He earns the title of high priest because he submits fully to God. Through Jesus, God fully enters the human condition with all of its pain, suffering, and sadness. Because Jesus is fully human, he can sympathize with our weaknesses (Hebrews 4:15).

Jesus sympathizes with us, feeling our pain, because he has suffered pain himself.

> In the days of his flesh, Jesus offered up prayers and supplications, with loud cries and tears, to the one who was able to save him from death. (Hebrews 5:7)

The author of Hebrews probably had in mind two key events in Jesus' last day. The first is Jesus praying. Following the Last Supper, Jesus went with the disciples to the garden of Gethsemane, on the Mount of Olives, to pray. He prayed that, if it be God's will, he might avoid the "cup" (of suffering). However, Jesus entrusted his life to God. (See Matthew 26:36-39; Mark 14:32-36.)

The second event in which Jesus enters human pain is on the cross. He cried out loudly in Aramaic, his native language, "My God, my God, why have you forsaken me?" (Matthew 27:46; Mark 15:34). These are also the opening words of Psalm 22, a psalm of the righteous sufferer. This psalm describes the physical and spiritual pain of one dying an agonizing death. Psalm 22, which begins with a cry of abandonment, ends with an affirmation of God's goodness and redemptive love.

Jesus understands what it is like for us to be on the edge of sadness; he has stood there himself.

Wiping Away Tears

One of the most poignant images of God meeting us at the edge of sadness is found in chapter 21 of the Book of Revelation. The visionary writer of Revelation, John of Patmos, sees a "new heaven and new earth" and a "new Jerusalem." He then hears a loud voice from the throne saying,

> The home of God is among mortals.
> He will dwell with them as their God;
> they will be his peoples,
> and God himself will be with them;
> he will wipe every tear from their eyes.
> Death will be no more;
> mourning and crying and pain will be no more.
>
> (21:3-4)

What a powerful vision of God's compassion!

When my sons were in their toddler years, they would sometimes fall down and hurt themselves. There was always a pause after the shock of the fall, and then would come the crying and tears. When this happened, I would pick my son up, hold him in my arms, and wipe away his tears with a handkerchief. This gesture would usually comfort him enough so he could stop crying.

The word *compassion* comes from two Greek roots: *com* meaning "with" and *passio* meaning "to suffer." To be compassionate is to enter into the suffering of another person and share in the pain. When the burden of pain is shared, it is lightened. Each of us can point to experiences where a friend, a loved one, a pastor, or a counselor helped us by understanding our pain and sharing it. This is what Christ does when we are hurting: Christ enters our pain and, in effect, wipes away our tears.

Sources of Sadness

Jesus' physical suffering on the cross was horrible and agonizing. However, I believe that his emotional suffering was just as painful. In the events leading up to his crucifixion, Jesus is betrayed by Judas, denied by Peter, and deserted by the rest of his inner circle of disciples. When Jesus is in Gethsemane agonizing over his impending death, the disciples with him cannot even stay awake.

Jesus was also rejected, persecuted, and hated among his own people. The religious leaders conspired to arrest him, tried him on false charges, and convinced the Roman authorities to carry out the death penalty. Could anyone have more reason to feel sorrow?

Often, sadness comes from a loss of some kind. When we lose a loved one through death, a part of us dies, and an emptiness is left in our lives. Life is filled with losses both small and large. Even the smallest loss can bring on a sense of sadness. The novelist Isabel Allende said in an interview after her daughter died,

> I finally understood what life is about: it is about losing everything. Losing the baby who becomes a child, the child who becomes an adult, like the trees lose their leaves. So every morning we must celebrate what we have.
> (Hornblower, Margot. "Grief and Rebirth."
> *Time*, Volume 146, No. 2, July 10, 1995)

In this statement, we move from the edge of sadness to the

edge of joy. While we naturally react with sadness at a loss, we can turn our sadness into a source of celebration.

Sow in Tears / Reap With Joy

Psalm 126 could have been written at the end of the fifty-year exile in Babylon. This psalm celebrates the "great things" the Lord did for the Israelites in their return from a foreign land and foreign ways. What brought the exile to an end, historically, was that Cyrus II, the king of Persia, defeated Babylon and ordered the exiles released to be allowed to return to their homes in Jerusalem. Indeed, the end of the exile was an occasion for great joy.

The central image of Psalm 126 is that of the harvest. The psalmist writes of sowing "in tears" and reaping "with shouts of joy." In my mind, I imagine tears of sadness falling from the cheeks of the exiles onto a freshly plowed field. Then, years later, I envision a harvest of joy welling up within them.

We too have experiences of sowing tears and reaping laughter. At a funeral, on the occasions when humorous stories are shared about the person who has died, laughter often breaks through the tears. Such laughter honors the person remembered and deepens the celebration of his or her life.

More often, however, the joy that breaks through our tears takes longer to arrive. The Hebrew exiles waited fifty years for the joy of returning to their homeland. When we experience a loss, it may take months or even years before joy can break through the clouds of sadness. Counselors refer to a "grief process" that we go through following the death of someone significant in our lives. It takes time to heal from such wounds.

Psalm 126 offers the promise of joy to those who wait patiently for God's strength and deliverance.

What Brings Joy?

At difficult times, joy seems elusive. No matter how fervently we seek it, joy remains hidden. The Declaration of Independence refers to three "unalienable rights": life, liberty, and the pursuit of happiness. But can happiness be "pursued"?

Pursuing joy as if it were something to be achieved is to fail inevitably to be joyful. Even so, our entire culture is bent on finding joy and happiness through pleasure, entertainment, success, and money. Yet, unhappiness is rampant in our society. In the movie *The Big Chill,* a group of old friends come together after the suicide of one of their friends. They are sitting in a living room discussing why their friend took his life. Someone asks the girlfriend of the deceased, "Was he happy?" Her reply is, "I don't know. How do happy people act?"

Like God's grace, joy can't be manipulated or forced; joy is a gift. Most often, joy comes indirectly, like a side effect. Real joy comes when we're doing something that is good and right and true.

At Advent, we sing, "Joy to the world! The Lord is come." Jesus' life, death, and resurrection are a deep source of joy for us. This joy is born out of gratitude for what God has done for us and for the world. God's marvelous love is a reason to rejoice and be glad.

Remembering God in Joyful Times

When we are living on the edge of sadness, it seems natural to turn to God for help and comfort. Painful emotions such as sadness or despair can cause us to pray for God's strength. However, when the time of sadness is over and we move to the edge of joy, we are no longer desperate for God's presence. The elation of joy can easily eclipse the presence of God. One story of joy eclipsing gratitude can be found in Luke 17:11-19. As Jesus approaches a village, ten lepers call out to him for mercy. Jesus tells them to go to the temple and pray for their healing. On their way to the temple, they are healed. They are overcome with joy, yet only one of the persons who were healed returns to thank Jesus.

If we're not mindful, we can forget God in joyful times. When things are going well in life and we are enjoying a success, a victory, or good news, we can too easily think that we have accomplished this for ourselves and neglect to be grateful to God. When everything is going great, we imitate the attitude expressed in the song "Let the Good Times Roll." Yet God is just as present in moments of triumph, ecstasy, and joy as in moments of defeat, despair, and sadness. Because of this, we can—and we should—give thanks to God in all circumstances.

"Again I Will Say, Rejoice"

The words above come from the apostle Paul's letter to the Philippians (4:4). This letter is the most upbeat and joyful of Paul's letters. This is ironic because Paul wrote this letter to the church at Philippi from prison. Even in a situation most of us would find discouraging and defeating, Paul was able to write, "Rejoice in the Lord always."

For most of us, joy and sadness are responses to events that happen to us. If we lose a job that we like, we are understandably down. If we are given a large raise, we celebrate. But Paul encouraged the Christians at Philippi to rejoice *always*.

Could it be that, for Christians, joy need not be dependent on the circumstances of our lives? What if joy is a side effect of our relationship with God, a relationship that transcends the changing circumstances of our lives? It seems that Paul considers joy as *in*dependent of circumstances and *de*pendent on a relationship with God through Jesus Christ.

If joy comes from our relationship with God, then we can rejoice *in* all circumstances, even those that are difficult and challenging. This does not mean that we are oblivious to pain or that we never feel sadness. To be human is to experience the full range of emotions. But we can rejoice because we know that no matter what happens to us, God is with us. The title for Christ that is used most often during Advent is *Emmanuel,* meaning "God is with us" (Matthew 1:23). God's presence is the reason that we can rejoice and experience joy even when we are on the edge of sadness and grief.

Repeat the Sounding Joy!

Joy is an emotion that is not easily contained. When we're filled with joy, it overflows into all areas of life. Joy begs to be shared.

In Charles Dickens' *A Christmas Carol,* Ebenezer Scrooge is paid a series of visits by the ghosts of Christmas Past, Present, and Future. After being shown the person he once was, the person he had become, and the bleak prospects of his future, Scrooge is transformed from a hateful miser into a generous and joyful man. When he wakes up from his encounters and discovers that he is alive and has a second chance to become a new person, he shouts,

> I am as light as a feather. I am as happy as an angel. I am as merry as a schoolboy.... A merry Christmas to everybody!
> (Airmont Publishing, 1963, page 120)

Can't we identify with Scrooge's elation in our times of great joy? In those times, joy overflows.

It is no accident that the story of Jesus' birth is one of joy. The angelic announcement of the Savior's birth that was made to shepherds in the fields, keeping watch over their flock, contains these words: "I am bringing you good news of great joy for all the people: to you is born this day in the city of David a Savior, who is the Messiah, the Lord" (Luke 2:10-11). These words are followed by an angelic chorus singing praises to God.

Christ meets us in our sorrow, and Christ meets us in our joy. Because Christ shares our sadness, we find comfort and healing. Because Christ shares our joy, it is deepened and increased.

Study and Discussion Questions

1. When have you experienced a "time of weeping"? What caused this time? When have you experienced a "time of laughter"? What caused this time?
2. What do you think was the saddest moment of Jesus' life? How was he able to bear the pain of suffering on the cross? How does Jesus' strength in suffering inspire you?
3. When have you received compassion from someone else? When have you been a giver of compassion? How does someone's showing compassion to us ease our pain?
4. What losses have you experienced in the past year? Which were sources of sadness? How can our losses be transformed into a source of celebration?
5. When have you "sown in tears" and later "reaped with joy"? How does Psalm 126 speak to you at this moment in your life?
6. Can happiness be pursued? Why or why not? In your own words, explain the following statement: "Joy comes indirectly, like a side effect."
7. Are you more likely to turn to God in times of sadness or times of joy? Why? When are you most likely to forget God?
8. Do you think it is possible to "rejoice in the Lord always"?

Why or why not? When have you experienced a joy not dependent upon circumstances?

9. When have you felt like echoing Scrooge's words of joy? Which brings you closer to God through Christ—sorrow or joy? Explain your answer.

Deepening Your Advent Journey

- Reflect on Psalm 126. First, slowly reread this short psalm, paying attention to the words and images of sadness and joy. Think especially about verse 5: "May those who sow in tears / reap with shouts of joy." Then, on a sheet of paper, write about a time of sadness that eventually became a time of joy.

- Think of someone you know who is living on the edge of sadness. This could be a person who has suffered a loss or is downhearted for some other reason. Show compassion to this person by spending some time with him or her. Be open to allowing this person to talk with you about the loss, if he or she chooses. By being a sensitive and compassionate listener, it is possible for you to enter into the pain of another person and provide comfort.

- Find something in your life to celebrate. You don't have to wait for a major event like a wedding or birth to celebrate life. Finishing a project or finding something that has been lost can be an occasion for celebration. Preparing a special dinner or going out for a meal or other special event can be two ways to celebrate. Celebrations are meant to be shared, so look for ways to involve family and friends in your celebration.

Fourth Week of Advent

Death / Birth

Scripture: Read Matthew 1:18-25.

Two Hospital Visits

A few years ago, I was making hospital visits with members of my congregation. On this particular day, I had two visits to make in the same hospital. The first was with a man who was near death. He had battled cancer of the spine for nearly a year, and the cancer had won. His breathing was labored and shallow as I sat beside him, holding his hand and praying for him. His wife of many years stood beside him with tears in her eyes. I could tell that the end would come mercifully soon.

After I left this man's room, I went to visit a mother who had just given birth to her first-born daughter. This birth came after several miscarriages and many fertility procedures. The mother's face glowed with joy as she held her daughter. We had a prayer of celebration together.

In a matter of minutes, I had literally encountered the two extreme edges of life: death and birth. Life begins at birth, when we are thrust into the world and begin breathing on our own. And life ends with death, when we exhale our final breath. Or does it? As we will see, like birth, death is both an ending and a beginning.

Birth: Endings and Beginnings

While we usually consider birth as the beginning of life, it also involves endings. A baby emerges from the dark and comforting warmth of a womb into the cold light of a delivery room. Leaving the womb is a kind of death: the end of total dependence on a mother for breath and nutrition.

Birth is the beginning of the aging process. Another way of putting this is, birth is the beginning of dying. A seminary professor once spoke to a medical school class about the role of pastoral care in hospitals. After the professor's talk, a young doctor-to-be asked the question, "Professor, have you ever held the hand of a dying man?"

The professor replied, "I've never held any other kind."

Birth initiates other beginnings. Birth marks the start of our increasing independence as we grow less dependent on a mother. With birth we continue to grow, develop, and change. Birth is our entry into the world of light, air, and all that sustains us.

The sacrament of baptism uses birth as a metaphor for the beginning of the Christian life. Among the first words of one baptismal ritual are, "Through the Sacrament of Baptism ... we are incorporated into God's mighty acts of salvation and given new birth through water and the spirit" (*The United Methodist Book of Worship*, page 87). Later in the covenantal service is a reference to Jesus' being "nurtured in the water of a womb" (*Book of Worship*, page 90). Baptism is indeed a powerful symbol of birth into a new life of faith in God.

Born to Die

During these four weeks of Advent, we have been moving toward Christmas, the celebration of the birth of the Christ Child. But although it may feel comfortable to focus on the sweet baby in the manger, we need to remind ourselves that the child who was born to Mary and Joseph is the Savior of the world. And Jesus fulfills the role of Savior by his suffering and dying on a cross.

Martin Luther's famous Christmas sermon "The Cross and the Cradle" proclaims that the cross is already present in the events surrounding Jesus' birth. In the Book of Matthew, the cross enters the story through King Herod, who ordered the slaughter of children under the age of two in an attempt to kill Jesus (2:16). The infant Jesus escaped death when Joseph took him and Mary to Egypt after being warned in a dream of Herod's actions (2:12). The threat of death followed Jesus even as an infant.

Jesus seemed to live on the edge of death throughout his ministry. That Jesus Christ was born to die is reflected in the comments of John the Baptist upon Jesus' approach to the river where John was baptizing: "Look, the Lamb of God, who takes away the sin of the world!" (John 1:29). Several times in Jesus' ministry the authorities wanted to arrest him but were afraid of the crowds that followed him. Of course, the authorities eventually did succeed. They arrested Jesus and had him put to death.

We too live on the edge of death. Not only is aging inevitable, we also live with the risk of illnesses and accidents. We don't know precisely how long we will live. Living means risk, uncertainty, and moving toward death.

Not the Final Ending

There is no denying that death is the end of physical life. The early Christian church rejected the notion that Jesus "didn't really die," because he was a spirit rather than human. The traditional creeds of the church affirm that Jesus was fully human and "was crucified, died, and was buried" (The Apostles' Creed, Ecumenical Version). When Jesus was taken down from the cross, he was unquestionably dead. Jesus' lifeless body was prepared for burial and sealed in a tomb. Jesus was as dead as you and I will someday be.

However, the good news of Easter and Jesus' resurrection is that death is not the final ending. Yes, it is the end of physical life, but it is not the ultimate end of who we are. Resurrection and eternal life are the final words about human existence. Not only are we born to die, we also are born to live eternally. A phrase from an Easter hymn expresses this truth powerfully: "Made like him, like him we rise, Alleluia!" ("Christ the Lord Is Risen Today," Charles Wesley).

A line from a famous prayer by Francis of Assisi expresses the relationship between death and birth in this way: "In dying . . . we are born into eternal life." Death is not the final ending, but rather a new beginning.

More Than a Physical Reality

In his poem "Death," Percy Shelley penned these words in 1820:

Death is here, and death is there,
Death is busy everywhere,
All around, within, beneath,
Above, is death—and we are death.
> (*The Poetical Works of Shelley.* Boston: Houghton Mifflin
> Company, 1974, page 408)

Death is pervasive. We cannot read a newspaper or watch the news on television without hearing of death. However, Shelley wasn't speaking only of physical death. Death is more than a physical reality.

Life is filled with "little deaths." These deaths are losses we experience throughout life. Moving from one city to another or moving from one stage of life to another are both deaths of a kind. The people and places we lose are not literally dead, but they are lost to us in significant ways.

The apostle Paul understood that death can be more than the cessation of life. He proclaimed that, outside of faith in God through Christ, we exist in death. This "living death" is the result of being alienated from God, a condition Paul calls "sin." Because we are sinners, we all "die" (alienate ourselves from God). But the good news is that through faith in Christ, we can have forgiveness and new life.

Yes, death can have a hold on us while we are physically alive. We can be "dead" emotionally or spiritually even while we are physically alive. There is a difference between merely existing and truly living. The gospel speaks a message of hope and new life to us whenever we are stuck within these "living deaths."

Birth: A New Possibility

When our sons were born, I was fortunate enough to be present for this miraculous event. After thirty-four weeks of pregnancy and twelve hours of labor, my wife was more than ready for these births to occur! The births of our twin boys were ten minutes apart. In a mere ten minutes, our lives were changed in ways we couldn't even begin to imagine.

A birth brings a new possibility into the world. In this sense, birth is the polar opposite of death, which is the end of possibilities. A birth opens up not only one possibility but a multitude of them. The word used for *human* in the story of the creation of Adam and Eve is the Hebrew word *nephesh*, which can be translated as "a bundle of appetites." In a sense, a birth releases many "appetites" or possibilities into the world.

With birth, a new life is launched into the world—a life filled with possibilities. A newborn baby is filled with potential that will later be realized. As a person grows, possibilities become realities. Birth is the beginning of possibility.

Being Born Anew

In the third chapter of the Gospel of John, Jesus is talking with Nicodemus, one of the religious leaders, about what is required to enter into the kingdom of God. Jesus tells Nicodemus that "unless one is born anew, he cannot see the kingdom of God" (verse 3, RSV). Nicodemus is confused by Jesus' words. Jesus was speaking of a spiritual rebirth, while Nicodemus was focusing upon the physical impossibility of being reborn. Nicodemus asks, "Can one enter a second time into the mother's womb and be born?" (verse 4).

Jesus speaks of this second birth as being "born of the Spirit" (verse 6). In the Gospel of John, several phrases are used to express this concept of a "second" birth, including "eternal life," "living water," and "bread of life." These words are attempts to capture the transformation from death to new life brought about by faith in God through Jesus Christ.

The good news of the gospel doesn't only concern the death that meets us at the end of life; it also concerns the "living deaths" that can rob life of its purpose, joy, and fulfillment. It is by faith in the God revealed in Jesus Christ that death is overcome. As Albert Outler wrote in his book *Evangelism in the Wesleyan Spirit*,

> By faith—and faith alone!—uptight lives are relaxed, trapped lives liberated, arrogant lives humbled, soiled lives cleansed, slouching lives raised up to tiptoe, empty lives filled, life unto death turned into life unto life.
>
> (Tidings, Nashville, 1971, page 36)

Faith as Death and Birth

T.S. Eliot's poem "Journey of the Magi" describes the journey of the wise men as difficult and arduous. The Magi have to endure cold weather, surly camel drivers, hostile cities, and lack of sleep. They finally arrive to behold the Christ and worship him. However, this encounter with Christ changes them, and they are no longer content to worship their former gods. Toward the end of the poem, the narrator asks, "Were we lead all that way for Birth or Death?"

The "Journey of the Magi" poetically describes Eliot's conversion to Christianity as an adult. His belief in Jesus Christ came at the end of a long struggle, which involved both birth and death. Conversion is a birth because it is the beginning of a new relationship with God and a new way of life. However, conversion is a death because it means dying to a former way of life. The apostle Paul put it this way:

> I have been crucified with Christ; and it is no longer I who live, but it is Christ who lives in me. And the life I now live in the flesh I live by faith in the Son of God, who loved me and gave himself for me.
>
> (Galatians 2:19-20)

Putting our whole trust in Christ means dying in some ways and being born in others. Baptism is a powerful symbol of this death and birth. To go under the water is a kind of death because we are deprived of air. Being raised out of the water is like being born into light and air. No wonder Paul described baptism as dying with Christ and being "raised from the dead" (Romans 6:2-4).

Jesus' Birth, Our Rebirth

In a compact and concise manner, Matthew 1:18-25 retells the events leading up to and including Jesus' birth. The entire Nativity story is told in only seven sentences. However, each sentence is packed with meaning—especially verse 21. In this verse, Joseph is told by an angel of the Lord, "She [Mary] will bear a son, and you are to name him Jesus, for he will save his people from their sins."

This verse points to the unique nature of Jesus' birth. This birth introduces an amazing possibility into the world—the possibility of redemption. A Savior was born in Bethlehem, the Savior of the world.

Several Christmas carols capture the saving nature of Jesus' birth. These hymns express this saving nature as the possibility that Jesus is born *in us*. The fourth verse of "O Little Town of Bethlehem" begins this way:

> O holy Child of Bethlehem,
> descend to us, we pray;
> cast out our sin, and enter in,
> be born in us today.
>   (Phillips Brooks, ca. 1868)

Charles Wesley's rousing "Hark! the Herald Angels Sing" contains these words:

> Mild he lays his glory by,
> born that we no more may die,
> born to raise us from the earth,
> born to give us second birth.
>   (1739)

These and other hymn writers have used the poetry of our faith to express the truth that Jesus' birth means the possibility of our rebirth. They underline the fact that Jesus' birth offers a saving possibility to us.

Emmanuel: Christ at the Edges of Life

For the past four weeks, we have explored the extremes of promise / fulfillment; despair / hope; sadness / joy; and death / birth. At each of the edges of life, we have seen how Christ is with us. In the negative edges, Christ gives us strength and support and shares our suffering. In the positive edges, Christ celebrates with us.

In Matthew 1:23, Jesus is called *Emmanuel*, which is translated as "God is with us." This is a fitting summary for the key message of this study: Through Jesus Christ, "God is with us" in all of life. God is with us at the outer edges, when hope seems lost and despair has triumphed. God is with us in the high moments of life, when all seems right with the world. And God is with us between these extremes, where most of life is lived—in the routines and tasks that make up our days. In Christ, *Emmanuel:* God is with us. This is worth celebrating not only at Christmas, but every day of the year.

Study and Discussion Questions

1. When have you encountered death and birth in close proximity? How did—or how might—you react to each of these edges?
2. How does birth involve both endings and beginnings? In what ways is baptism a kind of birth?
3. Where do you see the cross in the cradle? How is the cross a part of Jesus' entire ministry? How do you deal with the knowledge that you "live on the edge of death"?
4. Why is death not the final ending? How does your faith in God through Christ reassure you of eternal life?
5. How can death be understood as more than the physical end of life? When have you existed in a "living death"?
6. What possibilities came into being at your birth? Do you think that "a bundle of appetites" is a good definition of a person? Why or why not?
7. What does Jesus mean by being "born anew"? In the words of Albert Outler, "By faith—and faith alone!—uptight lives are relaxed, trapped lives liberated, arrogant lives humbled, soiled lives cleansed, slouching lives raised up to tiptoe, empty lives filled, life unto death turned into life unto life." What do these words say about death and rebirth?
8. In what ways is faith in Christ a birth? In what ways is

faith in Christ a death? How does conversion to the Christian faith involve both birth and death?

9. How can a birth that took place over 2,000 years ago have any influence on us today? How does Jesus' birth introduce a saving possibility into our world?

Deepening Your Advent Journey

- The fourth week of Advent ends with the celebration of Christmas. Often, we sing Christmas hymns and carols on the fourth Sunday of Advent, as well as at church services on Christmas Eve and Christmas Sunday. This week, carefully read the verses of these Christmas hymns as they appear in your hymnal or songbook. As you read the poetry of these hymns and carols, pay attention to how the words *birth* and *death* are used. Take time to reflect on the meaning of Jesus' birth for your life.

- Read Romans 6:1-14. In this section, Paul presents the Christian life as one of "dying" and "rising" with Christ. Fold a sheet of paper in half and write these questions at the top, making two separate columns: (1) In what ways have I died with Christ? (2) How have I been raised to a new life through faith in Christ? Then, make a list of answers under each question.

- In the hymn "Joy to the World" is the phrase "Let every heart prepare him room." This week, find ways to prepare your heart for Christmas. There are several ways to do this, such as reading a favorite Christmas story or watching a favorite Christmas movie, listening to Christmas carols, making time for prayer and meditation each day, reaching out to someone who needs what you can offer, or taking a walk to reflect on the meaning of Christmas. Use your creativity and imagination, allowing God to speak to you in a personal way as you prepare room in your heart for Jesus Christ at Christmastime and throughout the year.